Our Government

by Ellen Bari

Table of Contents

Introduction 2

Chapter 1
National Government: The Executive Branch 4

Chapter 2
National Government: The Legislative Branch 10

Chapter 3
National Government: The Judicial Branch 14

Chapter 4
State Government 16

Chapter 5
Local Government 18

Conclusion 22

Glossary 23

Index 24

Introduction

What does the president of the United States do? Who makes up the laws in your state? Who decides to put a new traffic light near your school? The answers to those questions have to do with different kinds of government.

There is one national government in Washington, D.C., that takes care of the whole country. There is a state government for each state. And there are local governments in cities and towns across America.

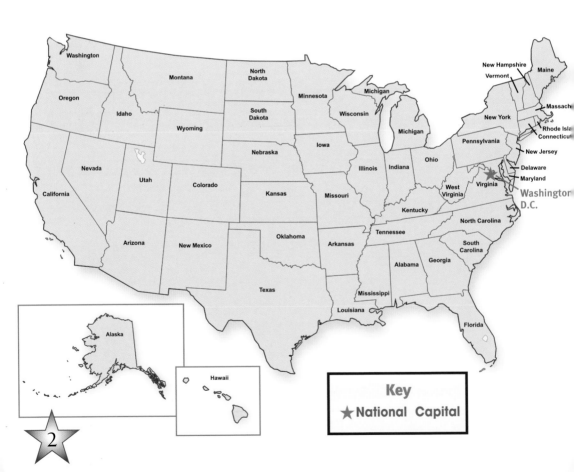

Key
★ National Capital

▲ Citizens vote for people who work in different levels of government.

In this book you will learn about government in the United States. It is called a **democracy** (deh-MOCK-ruh-see). In a democracy, **citizens** decide what the government can do. Citizens are people who are born in a country, or who choose to become a member of a country. Citizens make sure that governments work to protect people's rights, or freedoms.

Read on to find out how citizens help make government in the United States. You will learn what these governments do for all of us.

National Government
The Executive Branch

The national government has three branches, or parts. Each branch has different jobs.

- The **executive** (ig-ZEH-kyuh-tiv) **branch** makes sure that laws are followed.

- The **legislative** (LEJ-is-lay-tiv) **branch** makes laws.

- The **judicial** (joo-DISH-uhl) **branch** makes sure that laws are fair to all people.

In this chapter, you will read about the executive branch.

▼ Washington, D.C., is our nation's capital.

The president of the United States is the head of the executive branch. The president is **elected** to serve for four years. The president has many different jobs. The president must be at least thirty-five years old. He or she must be a citizen who was born in the United States. He or she must have lived in the United States for at least fourteen years.

Official Titles of the President

Title	Duties
Chief Executive	• Runs the government • Makes sure laws are followed
Chief of State	• Speaks and acts for the United States to the rest of the world
Commander-in-Chief	• Is in charge of the military, or armed forces

Each day, the president makes important decisions for the country.

The president appoints, or chooses, a number of men and women to help make these decisions.

They are called the **Cabinet**. Each Cabinet member advises the president about one special area.

▲ President George W. Bush and Condoleeza Rice, a member of the president's Cabinet

Primary Source

Presidential Oath "I do solemnly swear that I will faithfully execute the Office of President of the United States, and will to the best of my ability, preserve, protect, and defend the Constitution of the United States."

George Washington took this oath, or promise, when he became the first president. Since then, every president has taken the same oath.

Historical Perspective

Today, all citizens of the United States have the right to vote. But it was not always that way. It took many years for African Americans and women to get the right to vote.

Primary Source

John Adams was the second president of the United States. He served from 1797 to 1801. He and his wife Abigail wrote many letters to each other when they were apart.

Abigail believed that women should have equal rights in the new country. This included the right vote. This is from a letter Abigail wrote to John on March 31, 1776:

"If care and attention is not paid to the ladies, we . . . will not hold ourselves bound by any laws in which we have no voice, or Representation . . ."

Time Line of Voting Rights

1789	1870
The first election for president of the United States is held. Only white men who own property can vote.	African American men get the right to vote.

The president lives and works in the White House. The White House is on eighteen acres of land. The White House has a bowling alley, a swimming pool, and a movie theater. Why is the White House so white? Every four years, it gets a fresh coat of white paint!

1. Solve This

The White House has 6 floors and 132 rooms. It has 147 windows, 412 doors, 12 chimneys, 7 staircases, and 3 elevators. If you were asked to buy a can of paint for every chimney, door, and staircase, how many cans of paint would you need?

A law is passed stating that all voters must be treated fairly. Voters cannot be required to pass a reading test.

Women get the right to vote.

Citizens who do not speak English get the right to vote.

| 1920 | 1965 | 1971 | 1975 |

The voting age is lowered from 21 years of age to 18 years of age.

9

National Government
The Legislative Branch

The legislative branch of the national government is **Congress**. Congress is made up of the Senate and the House of Representatives. Congress makes the laws for our nation.

Every state elects people to serve in the Senate and the House of Representatives. These people are chosen to speak for the citizens in the states.

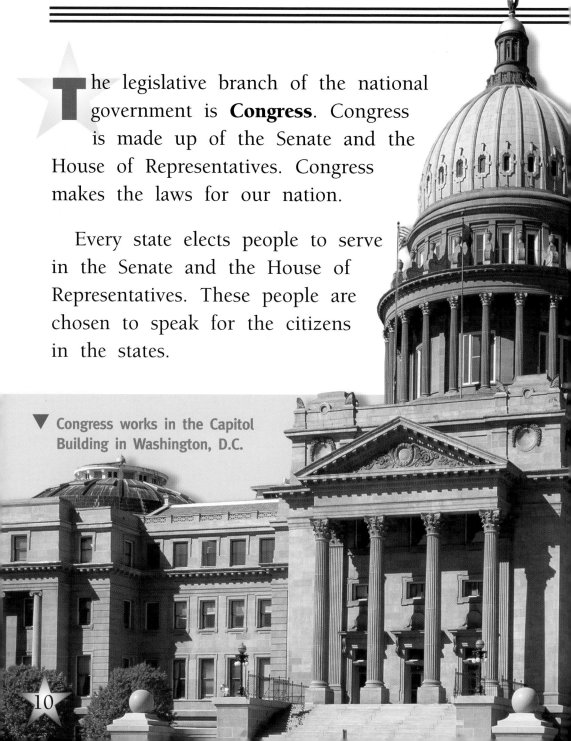

▼ Congress works in the Capitol Building in Washington, D.C.

The Senate

The elected members of the Senate are called senators. There are 100 senators in the Senate. Each state has two senators.

Senators are elected to office for a term of six years. They can be re-elected again and again.

President Barack Obama

In 2008, Barack Obama (buh-ROCK oh-BAH-muh), a senator from Illinois, was elected president of the United States. He became the first African American to hold the position.

Mr. Obama has always tried to improve the lives of the poor, and the lives of working families. He has fought hard for better schools and health care.

The House of Representatives

The members of the House of Representatives are called representatives. There are 435 representatives in the House. The number of representatives a state has depends on the number of people who live in the state. For example, Wyoming does not have many people. It has one representative. Texas, with many people, has thirty-two representatives.

Representatives are elected for a term of two years. They can be re-elected again and again.

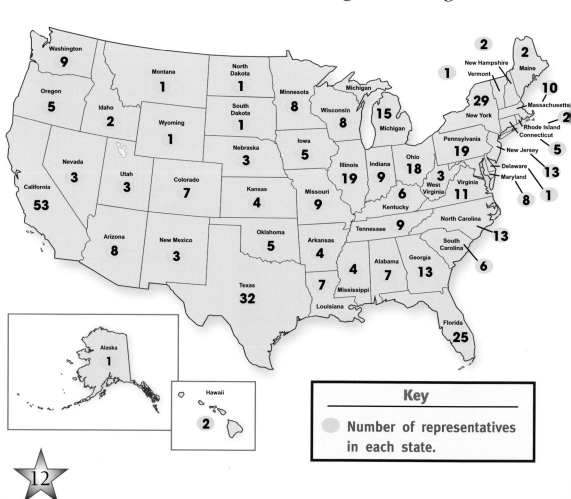

Key

Number of representatives in each state.

▲ U.S. representatives are elected to serve two years in Congress.

Each representative comes from a district, or area, in his or her state. Representatives work on problems that are important to the people in their districts.

2. Solve This

This bar graph shows the number of representatives from three states.

a. Which state shown in the graph has the most members in the House of Representatives?

b. Which state has the least members?

c. About how many more members does California have than Texas?

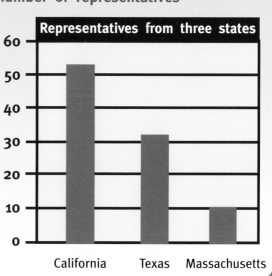

Representatives from three states

California   Texas   Massachusetts

13

CHAPTER 3

National Government
The Judicial Branch

The judicial branch of the national government is made up of nine people called **justices** (JUS-tih-sez). They meet together as the United States Supreme (soo-PREEM) Court. The justices decide if laws are fair.

United States Supreme Court, 2004 ▶

In 1981, Sandra Day O'Connor made history. She became the first woman ever appointed as a Supreme Court justice. In 2005, Justice O'Connor announced her plans to retire.

To be fair, laws must obey the Constitution of the United States. The justices can decide if laws do not agree with the Constitution.

▲ John Roberts became the seventeenth Chief Justice on September 29, 2005.

✓ POINT

Reread

Reread pages 14–15. What is the Supreme Court? What role does it play in our national government?

CHAPTER 4

State Government

Each state has a government. Each state government has three branches. All three branches work together to run the state.

The **governor** is head of the executive branch. The governor's most important job is to carry out state laws.

The lawmakers write new laws that they think will help their state. They are the legislative branch.

The third branch is called the judicial branch. It is made up of the state courts. Judges in state courts make sure laws are fair.

Each governor on the chart below became a president of the United States. Study the chart and answer the questions.

a. Which president served as governor for the longest time? How many years did he serve as governor?

b. Which president served as governor for the shortest time? How many years did he serve as governor?

Governor	Jimmy Carter	Ronald Reagan	Bill Clinton	George W. Bush

State	Georgia	California	Arkansas	Texas
Years	1971–1975	1967–1975	1979–1981 1983–1992	1994–2000

▼ State Capitol Building in Austin, Texas

Local Government

There is one national government. There are fifty state governments. But there are thousands of local governments!

Some governments in very small communities have town meetings. People go to town meetings to talk about their communities. They vote on what to do for the communities.

In bigger towns and cities, citizens elect people to represent them in local government. Citizens vote for these people.

▼ city council session

JOHN J. HAMILTON, JR. COUNCILMAN

JOHN M. LOFFREDO COUNCILMAN

City Government

A **mayor** is the leader of a city's government. The mayor makes sure the city government runs well.

In almost all cities, the mayor works with a city **council**. A council is a group of people who make laws. Citizens elect the city council.

▲ Rudy Giuliani was the mayor of New York City from 1993–2001.

County Government

Most states are divided into counties. A **county** is an area of a state that includes several communities. People who live in a county vote for the people in the county government. The leaders of county governments are officials such as sheriffs and commissioners (kuh-MISH-uh-nurs).

Sheriffs protect citizens and make sure laws are obeyed.

Local Government in Action

Local government makes laws. It also provides services to citizens. Police officers, firefighters, and crossing guards provide the services.

How does local government pay for all of the services? Citizens and businesses pay taxes to the local government. The local government then decides how much money goes to each service. People do not always agree about the decisions. But leaders try to work things out in the best way they can.

▲ Local taxes help pay the salaries of firefighters.

▼ Governments provide services like school crossing guards.

POINT

Talk About It

You have read about many different kinds of services local governments provide. What kinds of services does your local government provide? Share your ideas with a classmate.

21

Conclusion

Now you know how governments work in a democracy. Citizens may make decisions about national, state, and local governments. Many decisions are made by voting for government officials.

Each level of government has different responsibilities. The responsibilities include:

- making laws

- carrying out laws

- making sure laws are fair

- seeing that laws are obeyed

- keeping citizens safe

- providing services for citizens' daily lives